# Farming is a serious thing

A beginner's guide for you

Cynthia D. Rhoads

# Contents

Chapter One

# INTRODUCTION

Medical errors are the third biggest cause of death in the United States, according to a report in the Journal of the American Medical Association. Unnecessary surgery, hazardous drug reactions that rely on dosage, superbug infections, and other causes of death are all too common.

Vegetables are the most important part of any diet. Life expectancy increases with more veggies in your diet and decreases with less, and the opposite is true for those who don't include any at all in their diets. Basically, it's that easy. Many studies show that vegetables contain hundreds of essential chemicals that help fight or prevent virtually all chronic diseases and correlate vegetable consumption with decreased disease incidence even in cases where other detrimental lifestyle habits are present.

For two reasons, it's not as straightforward as it appears in the real world. Vegetables are expensive because they require a lot of work to grow, and because of the effects of contemporary agricultural practises, they are sometimes bland or otherwise unpleasant.

Although fresh (or at least uncooked) veggies appear to be less expensive than their cooked counterparts, this is not the case at all. A pound of broccoli is $4, a head of cabbage is $3, and a pound of tomatoes is $1.69 each at your local grocery store. Until you realise just how many vegetables you should be eating, these costs aren't that bad.

Just 10 percent of Americans ate enough veggies to meet the USDA standards for five half-cup portions (approximately two pounds) each day. It is also important to note that those limits are drawn from the USDA's recommended daily amount (RDA). According to many academics and scientists, the RDA for nutrients is sufficient to avoid evident symptoms of insufficiency, but it does not convey optimal health or prevent chronic disorders.

Vitamin pills can be used to supplement nutritional consumption, however it is widely accepted that they are inferior to food sources since they lack other nutrients that can't be replicated in a tablet form. In addition to enhancing the effects of the vitamins, these additional nutrients have their own set of advantages. A daily intake of 10 half-cup portions of a wide variety of fruits and vegetables is required to meet the nutrient requirements for optimal health. This is equal to about four pounds of produce.

There are four persons in your family, therefore you'll need twelve pounds of veggies every day, or eighty-four pounds per week. Even if traditionally grown fruit costs $4 per pound, a weekly shopping spend of $336 will be incurred only on veggies. Even middle-class Americans consume vegetables less as a primary food source and more as an afterthought or an auxiliary, in part because of the poorer areas' lower nutritional standards. Nutritionally dense, but not calorically dense, vegetables provide several health benefits. Vegetables are significantly more expensive per calorie than most other foods.

While sirloin steak costs $7 per pound, the price per serving of cabbage is just $1.69, and the calories per ounce of each serve are just 6.4. Steak has 168 calories per dollar, while cabbage has 60 calories per dollar. Steak and cabbage are both good for you, but comparing them to junk food like sweets or snack chips is much more depressing. For for $.89, you can get yourself a 3 14-ounce container of a famous candy that delivers 240 calories, or 270 calories per dollar. One of the reasons vegetables only make up 10% of the average American's caloric intake is their high cost per calorie. Because organic vegetables are healthier and taste better, they are less likely to contribute many calories in the average diet than conventional vegetables, which are less expensive per calorie than organic vegetables.

As a result, it is much easier to follow our mothers' advise if we raise our own veggies, as they are far less expensive to produce.

Most veggies available in supermarkets are unappetizing, and this is a major reason why people fail to consume enough vegetables. In order to avoid starving, humans have a natural evolutionary impulse to eat the most calorie-dense food possible. Our predilection for snack cakes over rutabagas can be attributed to this. However, modern agriculture has turned what should be a gourmet delight into something so boring and useless that it can't be consumed in large quantities without a dip or sauce to mask its bland flavour.

As near to an industrial process as possible can be achieved in modern farming methods. Every business, especially one that deals in commodities, strives to maximise profits by reducing the cost of production as much as feasible. The state of one's health and diet are unrelated.

Visiting a car dealership recently to trade in a truck brings back memories of that journey. For the past few years, I'd used synthetic oil, installed a new steering box, and performed a thorough inspection of the truck. It performed as expected, and that's all that matters. As a trade-in on the used-vehicle market, it was worth the same as if it wouldn't operate, had been neglected, or had its engine removed. To make a point, I'm going to exaggerate a little bit. What's the use of spending a lot of money on a well-maintained truck when it's traded in with a vehicle that has been neglected for years?

Keeping the truck in good working order was paramount to the comfort and safety of myself and my passengers. That was the only reason I drove it. It is a commodity that is traded at the dealership. Because everything is priced to appeal to the broadest possible audience, any added value you provide to the product is essentially thrown away. However, when it is for your own use, that value is never actually gone because of the value you personally gain from the investment.

It's no different in the agribusiness industry. You can submit a bid on bushels of maize, pork bellies, or tomatoes at a commodity market. "Brett's vine-ripened organic tomatoes lovingly grown in a soil rich in micronutrients" does not have a spot to bid. From a purely economic standpoint, if I'm going to get paid the same for my tomatoes as if I had coated them with poison and grown them in toxic waste, it's best for me to use slave labour, grow them in toxic waste, and coat them with every poison under the sun.

As a result, the vegetables available for buy at your local grocery are abject. Because they're so disgusting, no one will eat them! To make matters worse, the nutrients in their food have plummeted. For example, broccoli has 37% less calcium and squash has 52% less riboflavin than they did in 1950. The same pattern may be seen across a wide range of nutrients in the 43 different garden crops that were examined. Still, vegetables are healthier than snack cakes, although they've lost a lot of their nutritional value over the years.

Linux is a programme that you may be familiar with. The GNU Public License (GPL) governs the use of Linux as a computer operating system (GPL). In 1991, Linus Torvalds created the first Linux kernel, which was published under the GPL. Most servers on the Internet nowadays are running Linux, and a large portion of the fundamental infrastructure relies on GPL-licensed software. Richard Stallman, the founder of the Free Software Foundation, created the GPL. GPL was designed to make software that anybody could work on and modify in order to increase its capabilities or correct issues. Previously, software consumers were completely reliant on the vendors under a proprietary framework.

One of the primary goals of the open source movement, as articulated by Richard Stallman, was to create "software that works" The expression "tens of thousands of hits" on a search engine is now widely used. As a result of allowing end users to customise their software, it has evolved into more feature-rich and robust products. Even proprietary software developers are motivated to improve the quality and openness of their products because of open-source software.

“Food that doesn’t suck” is another significant reason to produce your own vegetables, according to Richard Stallman in the context of food. Vegetables grown in nutrient-rich soils can be grown to their fullest potential if you allow them to develop naturally so that they can be harvested at their highest nutritional value. Growing veggies that you and your family will like eating instead of concealing them in sauces or frying them to death is within your grasp, and you should use it to your advantage.

When it comes to GPL, you may also cultivate open-pollinated varieties of veggies from which you can store your own seeds and become independent of a faceless corporation located thousands of miles away. Alternatively, You can improve variants by customising them to your specific circumstances and need.

Another good reason to raise your own food is because it’s good for your morals. I’m not going to get up on my soapbox and tell you how to live your life; that’s not my job. Even though we share some core moral beliefs, I believe our media has done a horrible job of reporting on the current state of agribusiness in general. Aside from that, all I have to say are the following facts. In my opinion, it's more than enough.

When Ronald Reagan was president, he started the "War on Drugs," and I was just a kid at the time. Despite my own distaste for drug prohibition, something he said in one of his speeches convinced me that I would never use an illegal substance. By acquiring drugs, I would be helping to perpetuate the culture of horrible brutality, murder, and a contempt for human life that permeates the supply chain of drugs.

To say whether or not drugs should be prohibited or that a war on drugs is necessary is irrelevant. People are killed every day in drug-related violence, and I'm a part of it by purchasing the narcotics. Of course, it's entirely up to you whether or not you choose to make use of them. I'm merely stating the obvious: I don't.

So, what's the point of bringing it up now? Your hands will very certainly come into contact with produce from a slave's hands if you shop at your local supermarket, because the media has done such a bad job of educating you of this fact.

"slave" and "slavery" are neither hyperbole or literary devices that I am employing. "Slavery-like" working conditions, low income, long hours, and substandard housing are not what I'm talking about. Instead, I'm referring to real slavery, in which people are sold at auction, chained up, beaten, and even shot if they try to flee their captors. Even in the United States, it's happening right now.

In a sector where employers are permitted to hire isolated, non-English-speaking migrant workers at low rates and keep them in terrible conditions, the behaviours are difficult to pursue. Also, identifying the slaveholder can be a challenge. In the last fifteen years alone, Florida has successfully prosecuted seven agricultural slaveholders. In most cases, the only people who can be charged are those who were in the same situation as the slaves: underlings whose living conditions were no better. According to Chief Assistant U. S. Attorney Douglas Molloy, "ground zero for contemporary slavery" is the tomato farming region of Florida.

During an interview with Douglas Molloy, journalist Barry Estabrook reported the following: "When I asked Molloy if it was safe to assume that a customer who has eaten from a grocery store, fast food restaurant, or food service company in the winter has eaten a fruit picked by a slave, he corrected my choice of words. The assumption has been refuted. A fact is true.'"

In addition, growing your own food is a fantastic way to limit the amount of money you contribute to the exploitation of people in modern slavery. By diminishing the demand for slave-produced commodities, you are reducing the economic incentive for slavery. More than a thousand farm workers in Florida have been liberated by police in the last decade after being held captive and threatened with death if they tried to flee. People with no police powers may have a far greater impact on ending slavery on this continent by growing as much food as possible themselves. This is just the beginning.

As a result, I feel I've provided some persuasive arguments in favour of growing your own food. Slavery can be abolished by growing your own food, which is less expensive, healthier, and more nutritious than store-bought produce.

## FERTILITY IN THE SOIL

In my book, Mini Farming: Self-Sufficiency on 14 Acre, I wrote extensively about soil and fertility. Because good soil management and fertility methods are the foundation for making small farming an economically viable enterprise rather than a hobby, rather than only a pastime. Pest and disease problems can be reduced, yields can be increased with more density, food can be produced with greater nutritional value, and you can spend less money and effort to acquire more food with optimal soil.

Throughout this chapter, I'll summarise what you need to know, as well as provide some additional details. There is no alternative for reading Mini Farming: Self-Sufficiency on 1⁄4 Acre, but this synopsis will get you started.

## Beds with Legs

For a variety of reasons, I prefer to grow my vegetables on raised beds. Fertilizers are held in place in the soil in a live symbiotic matrix for release to plants at the appropriate time, and the soil temperatures allow for early working in raised beds that have been double-dug and enriched with finished compost. A raised bed's close spacing of plants also enhances yields over row gardening, while weeds are kept at bay by the dense growth of the plants themselves.

For small-scale crop rotation, beds can be useful. It's important to remember that each crop has its own unique set of needs and demands on the soil. Growing the same crop year after year in the same location is perhaps the most harmful thing that can be done in terms of pests and diseases. This leads to a buildup of diseases and pests that eventually becomes uncontrollable. Rotating crops minimises pest and disease problems significantly.

There should be enough room between beds to stroll between them in most cases. Sod/grass, crushed stones, bark mulch, or any other material can be used to fill the area between the beds. Between my beds, I have sod/grass, which is usually no problem. Botrytis, wireworms, and slugs can all thrive in these areas, so adding untreated bark mulch or straw between the beds to keep grasses at bay may be a good idea if disease problems arise. Grass that isn't frequently mowed can turn into a bed. You'll be raking up your flowerbeds by the handfuls before you realise it.

## Composting

Soil fertility can be maintained and even improved by the use of compost. In accordance with this law, nothing may be created or destroyed. Mini farmers will need to buy fertiliser if they do not replenish the soil with the nutrients that went into their plants in the first place. This is true even if you don't understand the physics of matter/energy systems. To ensure that the soil doesn't run out of phosphorus, it's necessary to restore the phosphorus that a tomato plant's foliage has received from the soil. Composting the plant, on the other hand, allows the phosphorus to be returned to the soil, reducing the need for additional phosphorus.

The aerobic breakdown of organic matter produces a complex and living substance known as compost. All of the composted materials' essential constituents, save for volatile nitrogen, are kept in the pile. Besides removing toxins and pathogens from the soil, composting creates a wide range of beneficial soil organisms that aid plants in utilising the nutrients in the soil to their full potential, and it can even produce antibiotics that can be used to treat disease.

Since it minimises the demand for fertilisers and prevents insect and disease problems, composting is vitally essential from an economic standpoint. Composting's importance simply cannot be overstated. Every 4 ft. x 8 ft. bed should have four cubic feet of finished compost added each year.

Chapter Two

# pH

The soil's acidity or alkalinity can be gauged using the pH scale. A plant's preferred pH range for optimal growth is determined by the soil's pH, which impacts which microorganisms thrive and how easily nutrients in the soil can be absorbed by plants. This is why it is crucial to maintain the soil's pH. On a scale of 0 to 14, the pH is measured. There are three extremes of acidity: zero (zero) and 14 (lye), while seven (seven) is neutral.

Many sources give a pH preference range for each plant, however these sources typically differ in the specifics of their recommendations. Tomatoes, for example, have a suggested pH range of 5.8 to 6.5, according to one source, while 6 to 7 is listed by another. For the most part, plants cultivated for human use flourish well on soils with a pH between 6 and 7, so you don't need to worry about it. Cucumbers can grow at pH levels as high as 8, but they can also thrive at pH levels as low as 6.5.

To ensure a consistent pH between 6 and 6.5 throughout all beds, it's best to test each one separately and make any necessary repairs before planting, as pH corrections can take months to show results and because beds are constantly rotated between crops, this isn't possible. When planting brassicas (like cabbage and broccoli), you need add more lime to the holes where the transplants are inserted in order to keep the pH lower than this. In the chapters devoted to various plants, these approaches will be discussed in detail.

For the most part, soil pH is too low and needs to be adjusted to a more ideal range for most of the country's crops. Because it takes several months for the lime to take effect, adjusting pH might be difficult. Despite the fact that the ideal season to start a garden is in the fall, the truth of life is that most people decide to start a garden in late winter or early spring. As a result, farmers are forced to fix pH within weeks rather than months of planting. However, with a bit of innovation and the use of other materials, both short- and long-term changes can be made to the pH.

However, I would only suggest powdered lime or pelleted lime, together with wood ashes as your liming materials of choice. Burnt and hydrated lime, on the other hand, can be dangerous to handle and can be easily overapplied. If you decide to make use of any additional products, make sure you read and follow all instructions carefully.

Pelleted lime is lime powder combined with a water-soluble adhesive for ease of application. The powdered product is no faster or slower than the liquid, but it costs more. Lime can take up to a year to take full impact, but it will continue to be beneficial for up to seven years after the initial application.

Calcium is replaced by magnesium in dolomitic lime. Up to one-quarter of the liming can be done with dolomitic lime to supply magnesium and calcium in most soils in the United States (excluding clay soil in the Carolinas). It is applied at the same pace as normal lime, takes just as long to take effect, and lasts just as long.

For a long time, wood ashes were overlooked as a soil additive for pH adjustment. Macronutrients like potassium and calcium are present in abundance, but they also contain elements like iron, boron, and copper. In terms of soil pH correction, they are more rapid, but their effectiveness is short-lived. For the same pH adjustment, wood ashes are used at twice the rate of lime, but no more than five pounds per 100 square feet should be put. As a result, wood ashes are utilised in combination with lime rather than as a stand-alone ingredient.

As with decibels, the pH scale has a logarithmic scale. As a result, the amount of lime required to raise the pH from 4 to 5 is more than the amount required to elevate the pH from 5 to 6. In addition, soil type has a significant impact on lime's efficacy. Because of this, the following table reflects both of these considerations The weight per square foot of powdered limestone is shown in pounds. Double the amount of pounds of wood ashes per 100 square feet in a given year, but never exceed five pounds in any one year. They work best when combined with lime juice.

Several sites advise against applying fertiliser at the same time as lime, saying that the lime will react with the fertiliser and neutralise it. However, this is not always the case. This is true to a certain extent. As long as lime is present, fertiliser will be affected by the soil. Don't worry, as long as both are well-integrated into the soil. Concerns about inorganic fertilisers like ammonium nitrate are also relevant here. Using organic fertilisers, such as blood meal or alfalfa meal, reduces the lime's negative impact on the plants.

Alkaline soils, such as those found in Alabama's Black Belt prairie region, are unusual in the United States, but they can be generated by excessive liming or by over-fertilizing.

Sulfur-coated urea, elemental sulphur, ammonium sulphate, and ammonium nitrate can all be used to decrease a too alkaline soil back to a more normal pH. However, despite the fact that these techniques are widely accepted in industrial agriculture as best practises, their concentration and potential for harm to soil biology make them unsuitable for small farms focused on long-term sustainability.

Aluminum sulphate is also recommended by certain agencies, although the aluminium levels can be taken up by plants and become harmful to plants and animals if the pH changes. So, if you're grown organically, I'd recommend either plain sulphur flowers or ammonium sulphate. As sulphur is 6.9 times as expensive as ammonium sulphate, it is more common to utilise ammonium sulphate for lowering soil pH.

Soil sulphur creates a mild acid by reacting with soil water. These water-soluble salts are transported away by rains as a result of this acid's reaction with alkalies in the soil. You can easily overdo the sulphur, so make sure to measure it carefully and adequately mix it into the soil to avoid creating an acidic environment. It takes around two months to gain maximum effectiveness, although benefits should begin to appear within two weeks.

By mixing ammonium cation with air oxygen, ammonium sulphate creates two nitrite anions (negatively charged ions), two molecules of water, and four hydrogen cations (positively charged ions). It is the acidity of hydrogen cations that causes the soil to become acidic.

So, how do you measure your pH? A soil testing kit or a pH metre can be used. In recent years, the price of pH metres for household use has decreased significantly, with accurate models selling for as little as $13. The instructions that come with your metre will tell you just how to measure each bed.

## Macronutrients

Plants require the most nitrogen, potassium, and phosphorus when it comes to macronutrients, which are typically referred to as these three elements. Calcium, magnesium, sulphur, carbon, hydrogen, and oxygen round out the list. Since water and the atmosphere provide the final three, they will not be discussed further except to remark that appropriate soil aeration provides beneficial bacteria access to oxygen. Water and the atmosphere supply the final three. Additionally, avoid walking on beds to avoid compacting the soil. The fact that raised beds are higher than their surroundings means they are less likely to become flooded, which is good for these helpful microbes.

The majority of soils in the United States are acidic and require lime in order to flourish at their best. Calcium is automatically supplied by the addition of lime. There are only a few alkaline soils in the United States, and they are mainly caused by the high natural limestone content of the soil. There should be no problem with calcium levels.

Among the many calcium-related issues you'll encounter is blossom end rot. Blossom end rot is a result of calcium absorption that is erratic, as a result of significant changes in rainfall. In most cases, this can be avoided by watering the lawn thoroughly. Calcium chloride, a rapidly absorbed calcium salt, is also included in certain commercially available formulations.

Magnesium deficiency is uncommon in soils where dolomitic lime is the primary source of lime. Even if the soil contains enough elemental magnesium, the complicated soil chemistry of competing cations, such as magnesium and potassium, might cause a plant to be deficient. It is possible for magnesium to become inaccessible if potassium levels are extremely high, or if the organic matter that forms the biological colloid that makes magnesium available to the plant is deficient.

Interveinal chlorosis (yellowing of the green between the veins) is a common indication of magnesium insufficiency in seedlings that have been kept in nutrient-poor starting mixes for too long before being transplanted: curled leaf edges that have turned reddish brown or purple. If you have this symptom, you can quickly remedy the deficit by adding eight ounces of Epsom salt (magnesium sulphate) per 100 square feet of space. Plants may readily utilise this type of magnesium because of its ease of absorption. It is important to treat the long-term shortage by adding suitable levels of compost and dolomitic lime to the soil.

amino acids—the building blocks of DNA and life itself—contain sulphur. As a result, organic matter is the main source of sulphur in soil. Compost-rich soils retain sulphur, preventing it from being leached out, and gradually convert it to the sulphate form required by plants. Even the most diligent composting, on the other hand, will not be able to restore all of the sulphur that has been lost due to the fact that food is rarely composted. As a result, sulphur should be put to the soil every year.

When it comes to altering soil pH, elemental sulphur is not a good option, unless it is currently being utilised to do so. It is unavailable to plants as a nutrient in its elemental form, especially in soils that lack organic matter. Garden gypsum (calcium sulphate) or Epsom salts (sulphate of magnesium) are the finest ways to add sulphur to your soil (magnesium sulfate). Either product has an annual application rate of 5 ounces per 100 square feet.

Enzymes important to cell energy synthesis contain phosphorus. Plant and animal excrement is the principal source of phosphorus in soil since it is in an organic form that plants cannot readily utilise. Microorganisms in the soil convert phosphorus to an inorganic phosphate form that plants may use. This is the greatest way to keep soil phosphorus levels stable since the majority of phosphorus is stored until needed and cannot be washed away by rain.

Phosphorus conversion by microorganisms is temperature-dependent, and spring transplants might suffer from insufficiency even if the soil contains adequate phosphorus. This is not rare. This is a problem that can be avoided rather than fixed by using an excellent liquid fish fertiliser at the time of transplant and every week after that until the soil temperature regularly rises above 55 degrees Fahrenheit..

Phosphorus levels in your bedding should be checked as well. There are a wide variety of test kits available, and all of them operate perfectly when used in accordance with the kit's instructions. If your soil is lacking in phosphorus, you should use bonemeal instead of rock phosphate. Adding bonemeal at least five weeks before planting is advised due to its gradual degradation in the soil. This will be determined by the findings of your soil test, which will be provided in the testing kit.

Since plants can absorb radioactive chemicals from rock phosphate, it is best to avoid it. Because rock phosphate fertiliser is used to grow tobacco, the smoke contains high levels of radioactive. As with peppers, eggplant, tomatoes, potatoes, and a slew of other garden-friendly plants, tobacco may be found in the tobacco family. To avoid swallowing radioactive chemicals, avoid eating rock phosphate.

In most soils, potassium is abundant, but in forms that are difficult for plants to access. Microbial life in the soil transforms these inaccessible forms so that plants can utilise them as needed. Potassium insufficiency is less common than with other vital elements, despite its necessity for life. This may not be apparent unless the same plant is grown in nondeficient soil and compared to the same plant cultivated in a deficient soil environment. To find out if there is a deficiency, utilise a testing kit.

The principal source of potassium in a micro farm is the careful composting of crop wastes. It's not enough, as crops that are consumed or sold cannot be replenished with the potassium that was taken out, thus additional potassium must be added.

It's a good idea to add some extra potassium to your compost supply from time to time in order to ensure that your plants are getting enough potassium. Potassium can be found in alfalfa meal, which is commonly utilised as a source of nitrogen. Potassium and other trace minerals can be found in wood ashes, which were previously addressed as a technique to reduce pH. As a mineral that formed on the ocean floor, greensand provides potassium and other micronutrients. Kelp, seaweed, and fish meal are all examples of this. It is possible to employ any of these materials in any combination to provide the soil with potassium that crops withdraw from it.

Amino acids and DNA in plant cells are both made up of nitrogen. Despite the fact that humans live in a nitrogen-rich environment, this inert form of nitrogen is useless to plants. Rhizobium bacteria, which live in symbiosis with the roots of legumes, perform nitrogen fixation, a bacterial process that converts nitrogen into a useful form. You may read more about this in Mini Farming: Self-Sufficiency on 14 acre. Cover crops and crop rotation, when done correctly, can lower the demand for and expense of external nitrogen supplies.

A lack of nitrogen can be seen in the plant's oldest or lowest leaves, which begin to lose their green hue. Because soil temperature affects the rate at which nitrogen in the soil may be made available to plants, this deficit is most frequently noticed early in the season when soil temperatures are below 60 degrees. It's possible that the soil has enough nitrogen, but the bacteria are unable to keep up with the crops' demand. Early seedlings should be treated with a liquid fish fertiliser until well-established and soil temperatures sufficient to enable natural nitrogen conversion. It is better to prevent this problem than to cure it.

Composting, like most other sources of nutrients, should be your primary choice for ensuring healthy soil. As a result, you'll need to supplement your soil with nitrogen as crops extract it from the soil, since you can't compost crops that you eat or sell. The use of legumes and legume cover crops in a well-rotated crop rotation can also be helpful. A soil test can tell you how much nitrogen you need to add to your soil.

In addition to manure from chickens and other animals that has been well-rotted for a long period of time and compost from an outside source, there are many other sources of nitrogen. To get as many micronutrients as possible, I try to use a variety of sources. The chicken manure we add to our compost pile lessens our reliance on nitrogen from outside sources, but this comes at the expense of chicken feed. To our advantage, the eggs are more valuable than feed, therefore we don't have to pay for dung.

## Micronutrients

More and more minerals are being found to be necessary to human health on a regular basis. According to what we know so far, the following are required: potassium, chlorine, sodium, calcium, phosphorus, magnesium, zinc, iron, manganese, copper, iodine, selenium, molybdenum, sulphur, cobalt, nickel, chromium, fluorine, boron, and strontium.

The only way we can get them is through the food we consume. If we eat plants, we can receive them from animals that have eaten them. But, ultimately, they have to enter plants through the soil. As a result, even if plants appear to be in good health, inadequate soils can have negative effects on human health.

There has been a long-term drop in the mineral content of foods because industrial farming does not have human health as its goal. A number of studies have indicated that in just a 30-year span, the content of vitamins and minerals in foods have fallen by anywhere from 6 percent to 81 percent.

Plants need a variety of micronutrients, which are substances that are needed in minute amounts. Because of overfarming, agricultural soils lack certain micronutrients because they were never replenished after they were exhausted. Only boron, chlorine, copper, iron, manganese, molybdenum, and zinc are officially recognised as plant micronutrients. This is due to the fact that plants normally exhibit evident negative symptoms when they are severely deficient in these components.

But since plants are our primary food source, soil shortage in any mineral essential to human health should be avoided, as the removal from plants means that we don't get enough of it in our diet.

Soil fertility and the retention of these nutrients are critical to composting. Mini Farming explains that these elements can be introduced to your beds in little amounts to some extent. Fluorine and strontium are more difficult to obtain, whereas calcium and iron can be easily obtained. It's possible you're missing out on something we haven't yet discovered.

In order to ensure the soil contains all of the trace elements required, ocean minerals can be added to the soil on a regular basis. Minerals that would normally be found on land have been transported to the oceans by rain and erosion over the aeons. This situation has been aggravated by over-farming without replenishment. Most people don't have the time or inclination to harvest kelp from the beach for their personal composting needs. A modest amount of ocean minerals is what I advocate as a way to ensure the healthiest and most strong plants possible.

Every known element, except those created in nuclear reactors, can be found in sea water in variable concentrations. A book titled Sea Energy Agriculture, written by Dr. Maynard Murray in 1976, summarised the findings of various investigations he conducted on the addition of ocean minerals to agricultural land from the 1930s through the 1950s. Despite the fact that his book was released some time ago, I've found that when comparing growing beds side by side, the ones treated with marine minerals generate noticeably healthier plants.

The fundamental problem with using ocean water directly is obvious: you can't grow plants in salt water because it destroys them. Even in ancient times, salt was used as a weapon of war since it prevented the enemy's lands from being fertile. There is no damage in using the modest amount recommended on the package, and in fact, plants become healthier and more resistant to pests and diseases as a result. Also fortunate is that the amount of marine minerals needed on a small farm is really low, so even 10 pounds worth from diverse sources will last for years. Every year, I use about five pounds of it. GroPal, SeaAgri, Sea Minerals from Arkansas, and more companies sell sea minerals. Be aware that each product is slightly different, so scale the package instructions accordingly.

In my opinion, sea minerals do not give enough boron for the micronutrient. Broccoli's hollow stems and potato's grey interiors will show boron deficit. You can get all you need from borax for the amount of boron you need. As a result, you should exercise extra caution while dealing with borax, as it is an effective herbicide that can leave your beds sterile for years. Before watering a single 4 ft. × 8 ft. bed, softly sprinkle a teaspoon of borax dissolved in one gallon of water over the soil. Once a year is plenty.

## Conclusion

Soil that is rich in nutrients is necessary for the growth of healthy plants. Composting procedures lower the demand for external inputs and improve soil health, both of which are important for disease suppression. Raised beds provide for better soil aeration, higher yields, and reduced fertiliser consumption in general. As soon as the soil can be handled in the spring, the process of amending beds for pH range and nutrient deficits should begin. Adding cover crops and crop rotation to the mix ensures that the soil is as healthy as possible, resulting in increased yields from your crops. Mini Farming: Self-Sufficiency on 14 Acre has several chapters devoted to these themes in depth, and I've just included basic information here.

# Chapter Three

## ASPARAGUS

You can eat asparagus without worrying about it being toxic! Toxic, but not the entire plant, are the berries that grow on the female plant. Urine smells a little different to the 22 percent of the population that can sense it, but these substances are completely safe. Folic acid, B vitamins, antioxidants, minerals, and vitamins E and C are all abundant in this superfood. The ancient Greeks, Egyptians, and Romans were all known to cultivate it.

By the pound, shops often sell asparagus that is past its prime because the stems have gone woody (so it weighs more). It's a lot more expensive per useful chunk than other options. At my local grocery, I can get organic asparagus frozen for $7 a pound. The low cost and high quality of store-bought asparagus should be more than enough of a reason to grow your own.

Asparagus is easy to cultivate and can be eaten fresh, frozen, dried for soups, or canned using a pickling method to keep it fresh for a long period of time. Asparagus beds can live for 20 to 30 years if they are properly cared for.

### Choosing the Correct Kind

Plants like asparagus are rare examples of dioecious species since they are either male or female rather than male and female at the same time like tomatoes. Asparagus is one of these plants. It's up to you to decide which asparagus kind you prefer dependent on where you live in the country. Some popular open-pollinated types include Mary Washington, Argenteuil (also known as Precoce D'Argenteuil) and Conover's Colossal. There are hybrid male-only varieties available as crowns (bare-root plants) but I'd recommend starting with a seed of an open-pollinated variety because it's easier to save the seeds and means you won't have to rely on a company that may have gone out of business if something were to happen to your bed.

### Asparagus can be started

Seeding Asparagus is a simple process. Plant it outside when your tomatoes are ready to go in the ground, around six weeks before the latest frost date on your local calendar. The reason for this is that only the male plants will grow substantial shoots, so start twice as many plants as you think you'll need. Others seeds are male and some are female. Six inches apart, place them in two rows on your bed. Keep only the two strongest female plants from the previous year to produce seeds the next year. After that, remove the weakest male plants from the bed and replant it with 12 to 18-inch spacing between each row.

Asparagus can be grown

Seeds or bare-root plants called "crowns" can be used to grow asparagus. As a crown is already established, it will produce useful branches a year earlier than seed-grown plants. Regardless of whether you start with seeds or crowns, remember that this is a long-term investment, and prepare the bed properly.

Drainage is the most critical consideration when setting up an asparagus bed. Asparagus is doomed if its roots become soggy. Make sure the raised bed isn't positioned in an area of the yard that gets flooded before using it. Secondly, the soil's pH must be kept as close to neutral as possible; asparagus thrives in this environment. As a result, the preparation of an asparagus bed and the addition of pH correctives in the fall should precede the spring transplanting of crowns or seedlings. Asparagus need at least six hours of direct sunlight every day to thrive. When planting six plants, you'll need a bed 4 ft. wide and 8 ft. long, which is 4 ft. wide and 112 ft. long for each plant. (For maximum exposure to the sun, place the long side facing south.)

It is also important that the bed has a good supply of fertility in reserve. As stated in Mini Farming, double-digging is used to incorporate adequately aged compost into the bottom of the trenches, followed by a good four to six inches of more compost being worked into the top of the bed. All of this can be planned ahead of time. To make up for any deficits in main nutrients that may exist, add trace minerals about a month before planting. Due to the impossibility of subsequently tilling more material into the soil, it is imperative that you only utilise organic sources when growing asparagus (remember: asparagus takes three years to produce, and the plants last as long as 20 years). Any additional materials will be applied as a top dressing to the compost. Five cubic feet of compost per 4′ x 8′ bed should be applied as an annual spring top dressing. It's best to put the compost in the ground before applying it and cover it with a two-inch layer of clean straw, which will help keep the soil moist.

Asparagus is a great source of arsenic, and it will provide it to you if you eat it in large amounts. Pressure-treated wood that has been treated with arsenic compounds is the only thing you should avoid near your bed unless you live in an old apple orchard that was treated with arsenic as an insecticide. Keep pressure-treated wood out of the asparagus's way, and avoid planting it in areas where arsenic was commonly employed in the past. Those who ignore this warning run the risk of collapsing in a heap on the ground after consuming only one asparagus stalk.

### Weeds

It's easy for weeds to build up over time in an asparagus plot, which can swiftly devastate the plants. Furthermore, hoeing weeds can mistakenly harm the crowns that create the shoots since they grow upward. Asparagus weeds are typically dealt with using flame weeding, mulching, or other non-herbicidal methods to keep the weeds out of the asparagus bed. Avoid allowing any grasses to get close enough to the bed so that seeds can fall there. The bed should be covered with two to four inches of compost each year, and the weeds should be kept at bay with two inches of clean straw. Hand-pull any remaining weeds to prevent them from setting seed.

In the straw mulch used to control weeds, you can see asparagus sprouting.

### Diseases

Several root-rot diseases can affect asparagus, although they are extremely rare to exhibit themselves in a bed of asparagus positioned as previously mentioned. Botrytis mould, which is carried by grasses, can also impact it, although this can be avoided with adequate weed control, as previously stated.

Asparagus can be killed by a variety of viral infections as well. It's thought that aphids spread them, but they're quite rare in homegrown asparagus beds compared to industrial farms, where acres of asparagus are cultivated. You won't have any disease problems if you just build a raised bed that drains effectively, keep weeds under control, and deal with aphids when they arise.

### Pests

There are many natural predators of asparagus aphids, including as ladybugs, that keep them under control. Aphids can be effectively controlled with two applications of insecticidal soap applied one week apart if you locate a high population.

It's more dangerous to have asparagus beetles. In most cases, they're a shiny metallic blue or black, but there are some orange varieties as well. The larvae of the adult asparagus beetle are the real threat; the adults themselves cause little harm. Green to grey wormlike larvae as long as a half-inch long emerge from the eggs, which look like black dots. Weakened by the defoliation, the plants suffer.

Cutting down all asparagus leaf when it has become yellow or brown and putting it in the compost pile is primary control for asparagus bugs. This prevents the beetles from having a location to raise their young. A vigorous shake of the leaf during the season will dislodge the larvae, and since they are unable to climb back up the stalk, they will perish in the soil.

## Harvest

Allow asparagus to develop for two years before harvesting if transplanted seedlings are used. You may do this by storing up energy in the tops of the plants, which will help them survive the colder months, Allow transplanted crowns to grow for the first year before harvesting. Only harvest the stalks that appear for one week in the first year. If you wait until 20 or 30 years from now, you'll be able to reap the benefits of spring harvest for six weeks. To restore the crowns, allow the remaining stalks to mature into full plants.

Asparagus harvesting isn't a one-time event. A stalk or two can be found here and there. A good non-serrated knife should be used to trim the stalks when they are no taller than eight inches. (As they grow larger, they become woody.) Make sure to put an inch of water in the bottom and keep the stalks there until you have enough for cooking or preserving. This method will keep them fresh for a few weeks.

## Preserving and Getting Ready

A few weeks in the fridge with the bottom end submerged in water will keep asparagus fresh, or it can be blanched and dehydrated or frozen. Asparagus is a great candidate for pickling. Despite the fact that pressure canning is theoretically possible, I do not suggest it because the ensuing mush is horrible in my view. If you're in the mood for some asparagus, there's no better way to enjoy it than fresh. The microwave can be used to cook frozen products if the package is properly ventilated to avoid exploding.

Tofu Pickled In Vinegar

Ingredients:

60 spears of asparagus

• 12 cup of coarse sea salt

Water: • 1 gallon of cool, clear liquid

Vinegar in its purest form:

In addition, you will need 1 1/3 cups of sugar.

At least 2 tbsp of coarse sea salt

• 2 tbsp. ground mustard

One tablespoon of dried dill seeds

• 1 thinly sliced yellow onion

• Four garlic cloves

Procedure:

It's important to thoroughly clean and trim the asparagus before canning, so that it can stand upright in a jar while still leaving an inch at the top. Add 12 cup coarse canning salt (sea salt is excellent, too) to a large bowl of sliced spears and cover with water for two hours. Afterward, drain and rinse the asparagus before patting it dry.

Four (4) wide-mouth pint canning jars and lids must be cleaned and sterilised before to using.

- In a medium-sized saucepan, combine the vinegar, sugar, 2 tablespoons salt, dill seed, mustard seed, and onion. Bring to a simmer after bringing to a slow boil.

Pack the asparagus spears in the jar in such a way that they're all the same length. Pour the pickling liquid to within 14 inch of the jar's rim, then add a garlic clove to each jar.

- Ten minutes in a boiling water canner with the two-piece lids adjusted.

All of these can be eaten fresh, garnished or used in salads; they're all delicious.

Asparagus with a Lemon Butter Sauce

Ingredients:

- 20 spears of fresh asparagus

Lemon, a solitary

A total of 112 tbsp.

- 2 garlic cloves

Procedure:

Remove the bottom inch of the spears of asparagus and wash and dry them. Set aside one half of the lemon for later. Garlic cloves should be minced. Add the butter to the pan and cook it over low-medium heat until it's melted.

Stir-fry the garlic in the butter for a few seconds until it begins to brown.

- Stir-fry the asparagus for a few minutes until it's soft.

When the asparagus is done cooking, add the juice of half a lemon to the pan.

The other half of the lemon should be thinly sliced.

Garnish the asparagus with thinly sliced lemons, if desired.

Delicious!

Chapter Four

# BEANS

In the garden, beans are among the most adaptable vegetables, and they may be used in many different ways. Tofu, soups, stews, and green beans can all be created from the beans, which can be used to fix nitrogen in the soil, as well as consumed raw. The cowboy carrying his stock of dried beans on a lonely walk and even small odes penned in honour of the... song... we often produce after eating them are two cultural images that are associated with these beans.

From traditional cultures to modern breeding, there are literally hundreds of varieties of beans available to consumers. Over a hundred varieties of seeds are offered by certain seed firms! There are many varieties of beans available at the grocery store, but the vast majority come from a few select cultivars, and the soy crop in the United States is 85 percent genetically modified to confer qualities like herbicide tolerance.

Beans are often overgrown, and supplies of dried beans can be several years old, further compounding the problem. The best way to get good beans is to produce your own, unless you have a connection to a farmer or can get them fresh. Fortunately, they are among the simplest garden vegetables to raise.

## Variety of Products

Many ways exist to classify beans, but for the majority of small farmers, bush beans and pole beans are the most common, as are the culinary uses for each (green beans vs. dry beans). Lima beans, cow peas (sometimes called "black-eyed peas"), yard-long beans, and a slew of other varieties are among the many varieties that fall under this category. The most important factor is the farmer's own preference, since they can grow everywhere in the country.

There is a huge difference in flavour and texture between fresh-grown beans and those purchased in the supermarket. You can tell a green bean is not merely a green bean by its colour. The Blue Lake and Old Homestead cultivars have vastly different tastes. Different members of your family may favour a different flavour of the same food. To get the most out of your garden, I recommend that you cultivate more than one variety each year and experiment with new ones while continuing to grow your favourites. It's preferable to have a variety of both fresh and dried vegetables on the table at all times.

You can start your own investigation by looking at some of the types I've grown and loved in each category, rather than relying on my recommendations.

There are various variations of this, some of which have a wide range of disease resistance, such as Blue Lake, Green Pole. When it comes to commercial processing, Blue Lake pole beans used to be the go-to choice, and it's easy to see why. Blue Lake's mild flavour makes it excellent for those who aren't big fans of green beans.

A productive pole bean, Kentucky Wonder (Green Pole) can yield eight-inch-long beans if harvested regularly. It's as if nothing ever ends! Rather than collecting the beans while they are still green, Kentucky Wonder can be used as a dry bean in baking and soups, making it a highly versatile ingredient. In addition, it is an excellent freezing bean with a particular flavour.

This variety's yields are impressive if you want to store a large quantity of beans. After planting, the beans are ready to eat within a week or two of sprouting.

Favorite Dry Bush Bean: Jacob's Cattle. Not only is it good for you, but it's also quite productive and thrives well outside the corn patch's perimeter. It is a white bean with purple splotches that is easy to harvest.

Bean soup recipes, according to my wife, should be made with Black Turtle, Dry Bush. It has a strong flavour, but it's delicious, and it cooks up beautifully. Despite the fact that it isn't as productive as other types, its flavour more than makes up for it.

It can be a challenge to harvest lima beans at the right time. As a general rule, you want to catch them as soon as they're large enough, but before they begin to mature. Its "lima bean" flavour is particularly distinct, with a touch of butteriness in the background. Steamed, they're a real treat.

## Preparing the Soil

Soil that is too acidic for beans to thrive should be adjusted to a pH of between 6 and 6.5 prior to sowing the seeds. Compost should be added to the soil to improve its fertility, and potassium and phosphorus levels should be checked. Soil nitrogen deficiency isn't a problem if you apply a bacterial inoculant when growing beans, which fix nitrogen from the air.

## Grown-Bean Sowing

It is possible to plant beans at any time after the last projected frost date for your area, by putting the seed one inch deep in the soil. Germination will be weak if soil temperatures are below 60 degrees on average. For a longer harvest, you should plant beans in two phases, with the first phase occurring a week after the last projected frost date when the soil temperature is over 60 degrees and the second phase occurring three weeks later. Most of the United States can expect yields into the fall as a result of this. If you reside in a location with a growth season of 120 days or more, you can even plant a third phase in another three weeks.

With or without an inoculant, beans will normally grow well; but, in order to maximise their utilisation as part of a crop rotation, an inoculant should be utilised. Increased yields are also expected.

A small amount of inoculant can have a big impact. You can put the bean seeds you'll be planting in a container, spritz them with water, pour in some inoculant and gently shake them about until all the seeds have some of the inoculant on them. Planting is done by planting them approximately one inch deep.

Bush beans should be spaced five inches apart all around when planting. Pole beans are planted on the north side of the bed in a single row, five inches apart and six inches away from the frame. Pole beans can reach heights of up to nine feet, making harvesting difficult. The bean vines can be pruned as they reach the top of a standard trellis or a trellis that leans away from the bed and is supported by a six-foot support. Either option will work..

## diseases, weeds, and other pests

Due to its rapid sprouting and growth, bush beans in beds rarely have a weed problem because of the leaf cover they give successfully shading out weed competitors. It's all you need to do is maintain the grass around the bed clipped and prepare the bed thoroughly before planting.

Bean bugs and Japanese beetles are two of the most common bean pests. As grubs in your lawn (or the lawn of a neighbour), Japanese beetles begin their life. Treating your entire lawn and flowerbeds with milky spore disease after the disease has been established for two years can be a smart preventative measure if you have a lot of land. The effectiveness of Japanese beetle traps as a pest control tool is debatable, as research suggests that they attract more insects than they catch, and that they may even attract beetles from the surrounding area. It works best for me if they are at least 100 feet away from the garden.

Beetles from Japan are attracted to one another. Picking them off by hand and dumping them into a basin of soapy water is one method of keeping them under control. If you don't use soap, your beetles will sink to the bottom of the bucket rather than float to the top, where they can scale the edges and return to your beans.) You can probably avoid the problem altogether if you pick them off regularly as soon as you detect them. As a last option, you can use organic sprays such as pyrethrin and rotenone, which are expensive and must be applied according to the manufacturer's instructions.

During the winter, adult bean beetles hibernate in the husks of the previous year's beans. A good preventative measure is to wipe out your bed at the end of the season and compost the plants. Bean beetles look like ladybugs with a bronze cast, but they're actually a little bigger. When these yellow eggs hatch, they form 14-inch long yellow grubs with spiky tails. It's not just the grubs that devour the bean plants' leaves; the adults do, too, and they're ravenous eaters. Bean beetles can usually be kept under control by raking up the previous year's plants, breaking any egg masses or grubs found under the leaves, and tossing the adults into a bucket of soapy water. This method does not work well in large-scale monocropping. Occasionally, grubs can be controlled using insecticidal soap or light horticultural oil (applied under the leaves), and adults can be controlled with neem oil preparations in the exceedingly rare circumstances where they aren't. Spinosad, an organic bacterial poison, is the most effective method I've found for controlling potato beetles.

Because of crop rotation and debris management, beans are rarely an issue in a well-managed micro farm environment. Sclerotina, a white mould that grows on vegetables, can be eliminated by switching to pole beans.

Harvest

Dry beans should be left on the bush or vine until they are brittle and tan/brown in colour, but not completely dried. Break open the pods and let the beans fall to the bottom of the bag after they've reached that point. Pour the beans into a large dish and toss out any large pieces of detritus. A technique known as winnowing allows you to effortlessly remove the finer particles.

Although mastering the art of winnowing takes some time and effort, the concept is straightforward. From a height, with wind (natural or artificial) blowing, it's possible to dump beans mixed with trash into a second bowl without any debris, and the beans will be the only ones in that second bowl. Use a fan on medium-low speed, a few feet away, and pour no more than three feet away from the fan. Using this procedure, you just need to pour from one bowl into the other a few times to ensure that your beans are clean.

To allow the moisture to escape from the dried beans, place them in an uncovered basin for a few weeks, stirring them occasionally with a hand. Then, in a cold, dark location, keep them in an airtight container.

As soon as they are large enough to use, green beans (sometimes called “snap” beans) should be collected. Flowers and beans will continue to bloom for a few weeks as long as plants are not allowed to overwinter. Interestingly, plants that aren’t allowed to set seed while being grown in this manner fix the most nitrogen into the soil. For best results, harvest the beans in an afternoon when they aren’t moist and store them in a bag for up to a week in the refrigerator until you have enough beans to eat or preserve.

## Saving of Seeds

If you plan to utilise dried beans in the future, you can just eat the ones you already have in your pantry. In this case, you’ll need to use the methods outlined in Mini Farming to dehydrate them. Treat green or snap beans like dry beans if you want to save their seed. Make sure you’re growing only one type of bean at a time and let at least twenty plants grow until their pods reach the dry-bean stage before you winnow them like dry beans.

the procedure for preparing and preserving

Plastic bags of green beans can be stored in the fridge for up to a week. Pickled, canned, blanched, and then frozen or dried are all options after that. They're finest frozen after being steam-blanched for four minutes and then cooled in ice water for four more. For many people, though, pickled green beans, canned or reconstituted from dry form are preferable to the way I prepare them, which is my own personal choice.

Green Beans from the Past

Ingredients:

• 1 pound of fresh green beans, cut into 1-inch chunks, with the ends removed

2 cloves of garlic

1 cup brown sugar

the equivalent of a quarter-cup of liquid

• 12 teaspoon of salt

• A splash of hot sauce

1 cube of bouillon cube chicken (use good stuff, not the bouillon that is mostly MSG or salt)

Procedure:

Slice the onion and cook it in butter until it is tender. Water, bouillon cubes and beans should all be mixed together before serving. Using a fork or spoon, dissolve the bouillon in water. Cook the beans until crisp/tender, covered, for the specified amount of time.

Chapter Five

# BEETS AND CHERRIES

The Beta vulgaris species, from which both beets and chard (also known as Swiss chard) are descended, is a wild sea beet that thrives in the Mediterranean. The greens of both beets and chard are edible, despite the fact that they are grown for their roots. Nutritional powerhouses such as beets, beet greens, and chard are an absolute must-have. Homocysteine levels in the blood can be reduced by the presence of glycine betaine in the roots. Because high homocysteine levels are associated with cardiovascular disease, peripheral vascular disease, and stroke, eating beets is a smart move.

Beets are also rich in manganese, magnesium, and iron, as well as B vitamins like niacin, pantothenic acid, pyridoxine, and folates, in addition to its other health benefits. A good source of vitamin K is found in beet greens and chard, which is important for bone development and minimising brain tissue damage. Other antioxidants, including vitamin C, beta carotene, and zeaxanthin, are also found in these fruits and vegetables.

If that's the case, I'd like to know whether they're palatable. Absolutely! The best part? They're one of the simplest crops you'll ever cultivate on your backyard farm.

## Variety of Products

Beets and chard may be cultivated almost anyplace in the United States where plants can thrive if the soil is properly prepared. Neither of these types has ever disappointed me, although you may discover over time that particular varieties perform better or grow more readily where you live. I'll provide you with a list of my favourite varieties, and I'm confident that you'll find them suitable, but please don't limit yourself to my recommendations.

Early Wonder, Cylindra, and Detroit Dark Red beets

Ruby Red, Rainbow (also known as five-colored silverbeet), and Fordhook Giant are all varieties of chard.

## Preparing the Soil

It is optimal for beets and chard to thrive on soils rich in organic matter with an acidity level between 6.5 and 7.5. Adding 14 teaspoon of borax (combined with something like bonemeal or wood ashes for appropriate distribution) per 32 square foot bed is a good suggestion because beets are particularly vulnerable to boron deficit. Beet and chard seed germination can be hampered by dirt crusting over the seeds, resulting in seedlings being suffocated. Uneven stands with varied maturation rates will result as a result of this. Make sure the soil is rich in well-finished compost to alleviate this issue.

## Preparation and Seeding

It is possible to cultivate both spring and fall vegetables, such as beets or chard. Temperatures above 80 degrees Fahrenheit (32 Celsius) might cause them to become bitter and harsh. However, beets are usually not ready for harvest until fifty to sixty days after planting. Chard and beets, on the other hand, do not sprout well in soil temperatures lower than 50 degrees Fahrenheit (11 degrees Celsius). A month before the final frost in my location is the best time to plant. During this time of year, the soil is warm enough to allow the beets to grow to harvestable size, but not so hot that the summer heat will cause the beets to become tough.

Successive planting of beets and chard is possible, but I've found that it's best done in the fall when the temperatures are colder and the beets are at their sweetest, rather than in the spring when the weather is more unpredictable. Plant your first crop seven weeks before first frost and your second crop four weeks before first frost for fall planting.

Seedlings of beets and chard can be transplanted into the garden after first being grown indoors. It's rare to utilise this method on a commercial scale because to the time and care necessary, but on a tiny farm it can boost production by allowing the grouping of more equally sized seedlings, thereby preventing plants that grew earlier from shading those that sprouted later. Seeds can be started indoors two weeks before they would normally be seeded outside, using soil blocks to hold the seeds in place.

Beets and chard should be planted three inches apart in all directions, regardless of whether you're using seeds or transplants. Plant them about a half-inch deep in the spring and keep the area uniformly moist until germination. Using a regular kitchen fork, gently break up the crust no deeper than 1/8 inch deep if it has accumulated. After germination, you'll want to trim out the surplus after approximately a week because the seeds often contain seeds for numerous plants. To make a wonderful salad green, save the roots and all of the thinned out plants.

diseases, weeds, and other pests

When the plants begin to grow, they will shade out the majority of the weed competition because to the close spacing between them (provided the bed was weed-free at the start). Hand-pulling the few remaining weeds is the best option.

There are few insect or disease challenges that are economically significant on the size of a small farm, but in commercial monocropping with inadequate rotation, there are several. After the previous season's crops have been harvested, raking leaves and mowing the lawn are usually sufficient efforts to keep issues at bay.

Beet-specific pests, such as leaf miners, spread through weeds like lamb's quarters, while more universal pests like leafhoppers and carrion beetles migrate from neighbouring tall grass. Either the illnesses build up in the soil over time from year to year's worth of agricultural cultivation, or they are spread by pests. So, if you just undertake simple micro farm maintenance, you'll be able to avoid problems in 95% of the time. Organic sprays such as neem or pyrethrin/rotenone might be used according to package guidelines to control the few that remain if they become a financial burden.

## Harvest

You can pick chard and beet greens as soon as they appear, but you want to wait until they have grown to a height of about two inches before doing so. Harvesting more than a few leaves from beets destined for root production can lower the crop's output. The outer leaves of chard should be harvested first, and then the following layer of leaves can be harvested as they mature. If you continue to pick the chard in this manner, it will continue to produce for at least three weeks. A plastic bag in the refrigerator can keep the collected beet greens or chard for up to a week until you have enough for preparation or preservation.

Beets should be harvested when they are no larger than two inches in diameter, though this varies depending on the variety. The leaves get woody if you wait any longer than that to harvest them (especially if you wait until the summer heat is at its peak). Pull the beets out of the ground by grabbing the leaf stalks slightly above the root. The leaves can be eaten after they have been cut off two inches above the root and the beets have been well washed outside with a hose. Prepare or preserve them as desired when they've had a chance to dry out.

## Saving of Seeds

They are biennials, which means they produce seeds in their second year of growth. Beets and chard are examples of this. It is possible for some types of chard to develop seeds in their first year of growth. Plants can yield seed the second year after being mulched with six inches of straw in the southeastern United States south of Maryland. The roots must be brought indoors for the winter and then re-planted in the spring if you live north of Maryland. Flower stalks of this kind can grow up to four feet in length.

If you want to save seed from your beets or chards, make sure you only have one variety in bloom at a time. It is recommended that you have at least twenty flowering and seed-setting plants in the population of beets and chard, as both are susceptible to inbreeding depression.

For harvesting, cut the stalk after most of the seedpods have turned brown and hang it inside upside down for two or three weeks to dry. Finally, use your hands to remove the pods from the stem and place them in a bag with the seeds at the bottom. The winnowing procedure mentioned in the chapter on beans can be used to separate the seeds from the smaller detritus. In a couple of weeks, dry the seeds in an airtight jar with dried silica gel or another desiccant and keep in a cool, dark area.

the procedure for preparing and preserving

Plastic supermarket bags can be used to store beet greens and chard for up to a week before fresh usage or preservation. There is oxalic acid in both beet greens and Swiss chard, thus they should be avoided together. If you or a member of your family is prone to kidney stones, you can prepare the beets and chard in a method that reduces the quantity of oxalic acid present. You can cook the greens by boiling them in a few inches of water until they're wilted and then discarding the water.

Blanching for two and a half to three minutes, cooling in cold water for four minutes, drying, and vacuum sealing for deep freezing are the best methods for preserving greens. Unfortunately, neither pressure canning nor dehydration preserves them very well. Dehydrating many greens is still an option, but I use my food processor to turn them into powder and mix them with spaghetti sauce or soups for an extra dose of nourishment.

Beets might taste like the soil in which they were cultivated if they aren't properly cooked. The "skin" of the beet, which is the outermost layer, must be removed. The beets can be cut, lightly rinsed, and then used in your recipes after the skins have been removed. Either use a peeler or cook the beets until fork-tender before removing the skin by submerging them in cold water, depending on how you want to go about it. The best procedure is the second one since it gets all of the dirt flavor-absorbing layer. This method of boiling beets preserves the root at the bottom while removing only approximately an inch of the top stem. Using a yard hose or a kitchen sink with a vegetable brush, clean the loose dirt before boiling.

Beets can be preserved intact for up to three months by cutting off the tops and placing them in a jar with a tight-fitting lid in damp sand or peat moss. When not in use, the container should be kept at a temperature just above freezing. When it comes to freezing, the end result isn't all that great. They become a mushy mess after being processed via a pressure canner. Dehydration and pickling are the greatest ways to keep beets fresh for a long time.

Beets can be dehydrated until hard after being peeled and skinned and then sliced uniformly, steamed blanched for four minutes, then dehydrated again. Beets that have been dehydrated this way can be used in soups and stews.

Preserved Beets

Ingredients:

6- to 8-pound beets peeled and sliced uniformly

Onion peels removed and thinly sliced. • 1 pound onions.

Lemon, finely sliced, 1 cup (rind and all, remove seeds)

• 4 quarts of distilled vinegar (either white or cider vinegar, 5 percent acidity)

A cup and a half of water

Sugar, two cups

the salt from the pickling brine

a teaspoon of cinnamon powder

Garlic cloves: • 12 teaspoon

The following ingredients: • 1 teaspoon of ground allspice

Procedure:

Remove the skins from the beets once they've been cooked. Slicing evenly is the key. Combine the sliced beets with the cut onions, lemon, and salt and pepper to taste. Add the rest of the ingredients to a saucepan and bring to a boil. Cook for 15 minutes before serving with a dollop of crème fraîche or crème fraîche and some fresh dill. Make sure that the jars are hot and sterilised before filling them with the veggies and the syrup. Process the jars in a boiling water canner for 10 minutes after adjusting the two-piece tops. Pickled beets will yield 8–10 quarts.

Chapter Six

# BROCCOLI, CAULIFLOWER, AND CABBAGE

During the first Bush administration, Broccoli made headlines because he claimed he disliked it. He may want to reevaluate his palette and plate now that broccoli, cabbage, and cauliflower have made headlines a number of times in a more positive light. The cancer-fighting properties of these delightful treats have been well publicised.

Sulforaphane, a powerful anti-cancer chemical, is produced by cabbage, broccoli, cauliflower, and other members of this family. Additionally, they are packed with fibre, vitamins, minerals, antioxidants, and other nutrients. My family eats more of them than any other vegetable because they're not only tasty, but they're also easy to keep fresh and can be included into meal plans with little effort.

## Variety of Products

It's possible to grow cabbage, broccoli, and cauliflower all around the country if you plant them at the correct time. They do better in the north since they are a cold-season crop that is frost-resistant. That variety can be grown in your area as long as the maturation date is no more than sixty days longer than the growing season (and most mature considerably faster).

Early Jersey Wakefield and Golden Acre are two of my favourite varieties of cabbage. Both are early ripening and have a delicious, compact head. Atlantic and Waltham 29 are two of my favourite varieties of broccoli. When the primary head of broccoli is chopped, both of these types produce a lot of side shoots, which have a typical broccoli flavour. Atlantic is normally planted in the spring, while Waltham 29 is usually planted in the fall for me. Cauliflower of the Early Snowball kind has given me the best results so far in my area. Our cauliflower crop is at risk because of the abundance of earwigs. The best chance of a pest-free harvest is with a fast-growing variety of cauliflower.

These are merely my own preferences at this time, and they are bound to change based on changes in the climate and soil. If you're just getting started, these are great choices, but don't stop there.

## Preparing the Soil

To ensure adequate levels of all nutrients, the pH of the soil should be adjusted to 6.5 and the soil should be generously mixed with compost. Micronutrient supplementation is especially important for broccoli since it is sensitive to boron deficiency. Before you start planting, make sure the bed is free of weeds.

## Starting

Begin planting spring vegetables indoors eight weeks before the last frost and outside three weeks before the last frost for cabbage, broccoli, and cauliflower, respectively. If you'd want to delay planting the broccoli and cauliflower, there's no need to worry; but, delaying transplanting the cabbage may reduce its yield.

The time of planting for fall crops is a little more intricate, but it's not difficult to grasp. Keep track of the date of the first fall frost and the date thirty days later on your calendar. Now, take the number of days to maturity for that variety, subtract ten days to account for dwindling sunlight, and record that day on your calendar.. On this day, your transplants will be buried. Mark the date that is five weeks in the past on your calendar. To prepare for fall planting, start your seedlings indoors today.

In light of my first fall frost date of September 6 and Atlantic broccoli maturing in 62 days, my anticipated harvest date is October 6. A total of 62 + 10 days before July 26, transplants should be placed in the beds. Five weeks before to that day, on June 21, the seedlings should be started indoors.

Also suited for frost-hardy fall crops like kale, kohlrabi and mustard greens, this method can be used.

## Planting

Vegetables such as broccoli, cauliflower, and cabbage grow large, yet they can still be planted close together in beds. Doing so reduces the competition from weeds. As a matter of fact, I rarely see more than a few weeds in a bed of this type of produce. As a result, plants should be spaced at least 12 to 18 inches apart. This will allow you to put up to 32 plants in a 4 ft. × 8 ft. bed.

Because soil temperatures can be too chilly for microorganisms to operate early in the season, it's difficult to predict soil nitrogen availability. Older leaves may become yellow as a symptom of nitrogen deficit in cabbage, broccoli, and cauliflower, which are heavy feeders. This can be avoided by watering spring transplants strongly with fish fertiliser every few days until they are well established and the risk of frost is over.

## diseases, weeds, and other pests

A well-prepared and weed-free bed is all that's needed to ensure that these large-leaved veggies can thrive in such close proximity. It is easier to hand-pull weeds while the plants are little because you may use a stirrup hoe to carefully remove them from between them.

Crop rotation and sanitation, like with other crops, are the strongest defences against pests and illnesses. Most disease problems can be avoided by growing in raised beds with pH levels that are correctly adjusted and prevent waterlogging of the roots.

There are a few pests that may attack cabbage, broccoli, and cauliflower. Cabbage loopers are the most prevalent. The green worm-like larvae of a mottled grey and brown moth are these specimens. The moths lay eggs on the underside of leaves in clusters of one to six. It takes only a few days after hatching for the green larvae to consume three times their body weight in vegetable stuff each day, generating an accumulation of excrement. They move in a manner known as "looping."

On a small farm, the economic impact of these pests is minimal because they only eat the crowns of broccoli and cauliflower and rarely burrow into the heads of cabbage. A rare delicacy for the chickens, I feed my own to them. In the event of an infestation, a Bt (Bacillus thuringiensis) preparation can be used as directed on the label to eliminate the threat. The nuclear polyhedrosis virus is one of many natural adversaries of cabbage loopers (NPV). NPV is killing any white cabbage loopers that are hanging limply from the foliage. Cabbage loopers will die in about a week if you can gather them in a can, wait a few hours for them to decompose, and then crush them into a water-based spray.

The presence of cabbage root maggots in newly planted beds might be a nuisance, especially if the beds have been amended with immature compost. The larvae of a fly that resembles a common housefly are shown here. Even though the plants have been carefully watered, they still appear wilted. Avoid using immature compost and planting no later than three weeks before the last expected frost date. Simply remove wilted and stunted plants, and you'll find white grubs all over the roots. Planting later and using only well-matured compost are the best ways to avoid this problem. Once this problem has been discovered, I have found that it can be treated by bathing in neem-pyrethrin-rotenone mixture to treat the roots of affected plants. It's possible that if the maggot damage to the roots isn't too substantial, the plants will be able to recover.

When it comes to cauliflower and cabbage, earwigs may be a real annoyance. With their large pincers on the abdomen, Earwigs look like something out of a horror movie, yet they're actually harmless to people (they can only inflict a tiny but harmless pinch). They lurk in the heads of cauliflower or the leaves of cabbage and inflict enormous damage from the inside out that may not be discovered until harvest. Although non-organic carbaryl/Sevin will work, I have not found any organic sprays that are actually useful in dealing with earwigs To prevent earwigs from invading beds, place dry pebbles around them, and trap them by spreading damp, loosely rolled newspaper near the problem areas overnight and tossing the newspaper away the next day.

Cabbage family crops are susceptible to a disease known as clubroot, which causes the plants to wilt even when they receive appropriate water. Because this disease cannot survive at a pH of 6.8 or above, adding a handful of lime to the soil in the transplanting hole can help avoid it.

There are a number of additional common illnesses that can be managed by composting plant wastes, rotating where cabbage family plants are planted, keeping weeds away from beds, and avoiding working in the beds while it is raining or snowing. Pretreating seeds (which may host some of these diseases) with 122°F water for five minutes prior to planting can help, as can spraying downy mildew with baking soda mixed with one tablespoon per gallon of water to treat downy mildew.

## Harvest

Cabbage harvesting is more of an art than a science. Harvest the heads before they crack but before they reach their full size for that variety. It's better to be safe than sorry when it comes to harvesting, as there is no such thing as harvesting too early.

As with cauliflower, broccoli has a short harvesting season. However, you do not want the broccoli's buds to begin blooming before it has completed its growth. (However, the blossoms are, in fact, edible). It is best to harvest cauliflower when the curd is solid but not yet gritty. Your ability to observe is critical in this situation. Every day, check on the curd to make sure it isn't growing gritty, and whether the florets open. Until you have enough harvested heads to cook with or preserve, store them in the refrigerator in a plastic bag for up to a week.

Use a sharp knife to make a slanting cut when harvesting cabbage, broccoli, or cauliflower. Individual florets of broccoli can be collected during the next few weeks for salads, and numerous mini-cabbages can be boiled and served as a side dish for a meal.

## Saving of Seeds

There are many plants in the cabbage family that can interbreed, including cabbage, broccoli, cauliflower, and kale and kohlrabi. Because wind and insects are the primary means of pollination, only one type should be allowed to flower at a time in order to ensure maximum purity.

Just don't pluck the heads from twenty or more plants in close proximity to save seed for broccoli. The seedpods will form if you let them blossom. You can remove the pods once they've turned tan or brown, break them apart, remove the larger debris, and then dehydrate the smaller debris using silica gel.

Cabbage and cauliflower are both biennials, which means they generate seeds in the second year of growth. Cauliflower and cabbage can be mulched with hay in the winter and cleaned off in the spring in southern U.S. regions with winter temperatures rarely falling below 20 degrees. When temperatures fall below 35 degrees Fahrenheit in the winter, you'll need to bring in the plants and keep them in a cool, dark spot, such an unheated basement. Gather twenty plants from the fall harvest and keep them in five-gallon buckets of moist dirt. When the weather warms up, replant them outside. Make an X in the cabbage's head with a sharp knife to aid in the formation of a blossom stalk. After the cabbage and cauliflower have bolted, they are processed in the same way as a head of cauliflower.

Seeds of this species are highly susceptible to crossbreeding, making it difficult to save seeds from more than one variety in a given year, but if you schedule your seed saving correctly, you may ensure you have enough seed to last for five years.

## the procedure for preparing and preserving

Wrapped tightly in plastic wrap, a cabbage head will keep for two weeks in the refrigerator after being trimmed of the base and outer leaves. You can store broccoli and cauliflower for up to a week in a sealed plastic bag until you have enough for cooking or preserving. When cut into 112-inch sections, all three freeze well. If you want to freeze, cut into chunks, blanch for four minutes, cool in ice water for four minutes and remove excess water, then seal and freeze.

Sauerkraut can be made from cabbage (as well as kale, collard, and turnip greens) using lactic acid fermentation, and vinegar can be used to pickle cabbage, broccoli, and cauliflower in pint jars. When pressure-canned, broccoli and cauliflower turn to mush, whereas cabbage holds up well. Fill pint jars two-thirds full with blanched cabbage, cover with hot water, and process for 45 minutes, leaving an inch of headspace at the top. Cauliflower and broccoli don't dehydrate well, although blanched cabbage works nicely in stews during the cold months.

There are many ways to use up those floret-free stems, including making broccoli-slaw out of them. After peeling the outer layer of the stem of broccoli, julienne it to make slaw. A 12-ounce bag of broccoli-slaw costs up to $5 in the produce area. Regular salads with broccoli-slaw are some of my favourites.

Cauliflower In A Baked Form

Ingredients:

Cauliflower, chopped into 1-inch chunks, one large head

olive or walnut oil • 14 cup

• 1 tsp. of minced garlic

• 12 teaspoon of salt

• 14 tsp black pepper, freshly ground

Procedure:

Pre-heat the oven to 450 degrees Fahrenheit (232 Celsius). Cauliflower should be cut into bite-sized pieces and placed in a big bowl. Mix the oil and spices until they are well distributed. The cauliflower should be placed in a single layer in a roasting pan. Bake for 20 minutes, or until the outside is crispy but the inside is still soft.

Cabbage pickled

Ingredients:

Chopped cabbage: • 1 gallon

• Diced onions, two large (optional)

12 cups of coarse noniodized salt;

The following is the recommended serving size:

This recipe calls for:

Water: • 112 cups

Mixed pickling spices: • 2 tbsp

• 1 bag of spices

Procedure:

A large bowl of cabbage and onion should be mixed together with the coarse salt, covered with plastic wrap, and left in the refrigerator overnight to allow the salt to absorb into the vegetables. Drain overnight and flush with new water in the morning. A well-tied spice bag is used to add the spices to the sugar, vinegar, and water in a large pot. Bring the mixture to a simmer for about five minutes. Stir in the drained cabbage and bring to a slow boil for five minutes. Remove from heat. Take out the spice bag and throw it away. Ten minutes of hot water bath canning is all it takes to preserve these pickles.

Chapter Seven

# PARSNIPS AND CARROTS

Mom always told me that carrots were healthy for my vision. As a precursor to essential vision-improving chemicals, the beta carotene they contain is unquestionably true. Vitamin K, C, folate, potassium, and manganese are also abundant in carrots. A member of the same botanical family, parsnips lack carotenes because they are white. In spite of this, they compensate for the absence of folic acid and vitamin E by boosting their intake of other nutrients, including B vitamins. In spite of the fact that parsnips aren't as popular as carrots, they deserve equal position in a self-sufficiency venture because they are both calorically and nutritionally packed.

## Variety of Products

Parsnips come in only a handful of types, including Harris Model, Hollow Crown, All American, and Half Long Guernsey, all of which are grown in the United States. Planting in the spring and harvesting in the fall are both long-season types.

Hundreds of different kinds of carrots are readily available, each with their own unique coloration, size, shape, and flavour. From the tiniest Thumbelina carrot to the multi-colored Cosmic Purple carrot, there is a carrot for everyone here. Carrots can be broken down into a few distinct categories. Long and tapering Imperator kinds, cylindrical Nantes variations with high sugar content but poor storage stability, fiber-rich Danvers varieties with strong storage stability, and Chantenay varieties that are short and wide make up this group. Many supermarkets carry Imperator-type carrots, although these tend to be some of the most unappetizing. This is one of my favourite foods. As a rule of thumb, I grow Saint Valery, Scarlet Nantes, and Danvers Half-Long, but I also plant a few purple kinds like Dragon. Carrots from Saint Valery can grow to a diameter of three inches and a length of twelve inches. As a result, they tend to be highly productive, as they can be stored easily and have a high germination rate for carrots. This variety of scarlet carrot has a blunt tip and grows to a length of seven inches. They're crimson, delicious, and virtually completely devoid of a centre. They offer a wide range of options for juicing. Known for their seven-inch length and ability to thrive in even the most difficult soils, Danvers Half Long are a market favourite.

Preparing the Soil

Deeply dug, free of stones, light, and with a pH of 6.5–7.5 is ideal for carrots and parsnips, though they can grow at a lower pH of 6.0. A soil that is high in phosphorus, potassium, calcium, and micronutrients, but low in nitrogen, is ideal for them. ′ Carrots and parsnips enjoy wood ashes as a potassium source. Make sure you use less nitrogen-bearing fertiliser than you would for other crops when preparing the bed. Animal excrement, especially, should be avoided in any form. As a result, your entire crop will be ruined by the smell and taste of manure. Because freshly applied or immature compost can impede germination and create malformations in carrots, you should always apply mature compost in the fall to beds where you intend to grow carrots in the spring. Deformed carrots are safe to eat, but they cannot be sold commercially. Deformities can also be caused by stones. While the carrots will still be edible and flavorful, they will be less marketable and more difficult to store because of this.

## Planting

Among the slowest-germinating crops in the garden are carrots and parsnips. Due to the difficulties of keeping the soil moist long enough for the seedlings to germinate, weeds are more likely to grow before the seedlings. Because they are so delicate when young, they should be planted at the widest possible distance apart to avoid having to be pruned.

It is recommended that these crops are planted three weeks before the last frost or when soil temperatures are above 50 degrees. It's easier to handle parsnip seeds than carrot seeds because they're smaller. Because of this, some seed firms sell carrot seeds that are protected from the environment by a harmless chemical that dissolves once the seedlings are moistened. They're about the size of a BB, making them considerably easier to handle. Alternately, you can have someone with smaller fingers take on the work.

A quarter-inch depth is ideal for spring plantings since the lower temperatures slow germination and cause seedlings to struggle to break through the soil if they are planted deeper than this. Late summer plantings can be sunk deeper into the ground.

When it comes to germination, carrots and parsnips take a long time, although this is temperature dependant. They need 51 days to germinate at a soil temperature of 42 degrees. It takes seventeen days for them to germinate at 50 degrees, but only ten days at 59 degrees. At 72 degrees, it only takes six days to germinate seeds, but at higher temperatures, the germination rate drops. When growing these types of veggies, timing your planting with the use of a soil thermometer can be extremely beneficial.

Using a fine mist, you should water the seedlings twice daily until they are firmly established. Providing an inch of water a week is all that is needed to keep them healthy after they are established.

Carrots can have one developing issue: green shoulders. Carrots' tops turn green and bitter when they emerge from the earth if they are allowed to develop naturally. If you notice any carrot tops poking through the soil, simply mound some earth on top of them, and the problem will be solved.

### diseases, weeds, and other pests

It is quite difficult to keep carrot and parsnip beds free of weeds when you plant them since the long period of germination can offer weeds an advantage. At this early stage of development, weeding can be too disturbing to the seedlings.

This scenario can be handled in a variety of ways. If you plant at 59 degrees Fahrenheit, germination will occur in ten days. Soaking the seed bed and then covering it with a board to keep the moisture in and prevent the growth of weeds is another method frequently described in gardening literature. However, in my instance, the soil adheres to the board and the seedlings come with it when the board is raised, whereas this may work in other cases. As an additional option, you can "solarize" your garden bed by soaking and covering it with tightly stapled translucent plastic a few months prior to planting. Weed seeds will not be able to grow in the top two inches of soil because of the increased temperature. Before planting, I go over the bed gently with a flame weeder to ensure that the soil is as untouched as possible. Despite the fact that it only destroys seeds in the first quarter of an inch of soil, this method is effective and efficient. During this time, I use the flame weeder to remove all of the weeds and grasses that have sprung around each of the plant beds.

Wireworms and carrot flies are the two most common pests on a small-scale farm, where crop rotation and cleaning up detritus at the end of the season are the most effective methods of controlling them.

Click beetle larvae are known as wireworms, and they can be a nuisance when they appear in previously sodded or adjacently sodded regions. As a result, raised beds are a common challenge for tiny farms because they are often located in areas that were previously utilised for grass. Carrots, parsnips, potatoes, and a variety of other root vegetables are all attacked by wireworms.

Grass populations can be reduced over time by using a mulch that smothers them, such as a thick coating of bark or gravel. A few days before planting, rake the dirt in the beds to encourage birds to consume them. Our chickens also get to eat the wireworms and other grubs we find in the soil when we rake it. You may also use potato slices on a skewer to attract wireworms by burying them two to four inches below the soil's surface. Dispose of the wireworms by removing the skewers twice weekly. Wireworm damage will be greatly decreased if the skewers are inserted into the root crop beds a week prior to planting and remain there for a week after germination. One skewer per four square feet of bed space is the rule of thumb here.

Another possible pest is the carrot fly. Carrot flies resemble houseflies, but with a more streamlined appearance. You may not notice them at first. They fly in and deposit eggs in the soil near the plant's base after being drawn by the smell of the foliage of parsley, carrots, celery, parsnips, and related plants. Grubs crawl into the roots and wreak havoc when they hatch. Because of this, you won't discover the problem until you've harvested the roots and begun to expletives.

Keeping the leaves free of damage and disturbance is essential in the fight against carrot fly infestations. This is a great way to draw attention to your garden. Weeding, which is the most common cause of bruised foliage, can be avoided thanks to the compact spacing of the plants. It's best to avoid weeding if you can.

Adding a few wooden pegs to the bed's corners and then wrapping a 2-foot-high piece of clear plastic around the frame and stapling it to the stakes and frame's edges also works remarkably well. When the plastic baffles the flies, they move on to a more convenient prey.

For the record, carrot flies (and certain lesser-known pests, such as carrot weevils) aren't fans of wood-ash-burning stoves. Carrot flies will be deterred if you use two tablespoons of wood ashes per gallon of water when you prepare the bed and water the bed every few weeks.

### Harvest

It is possible to pick parsnips and carrots at any time. As a result, when harvested early, the turpene-to-sugar ratio is in favour of the turpenes. After the first hard frost, parsnips become sweeter, thus they should be harvested at this time. It is best not to leave carrots in the ground for more than two weeks after the stated maturity date of that variety, as this can lead to their becoming fibrous.

Carrots and parsnips can be harvested by soaking the roots thoroughly in water, grasping the foliage as close to the base as possible, and pulling while twisting. Dig gently around the affected roots if the tops break off with a digging fork or hand shovel. Place the tops in the compost pile immediately after cutting them off about a quarter inch above the root. Allow the dirt on the roots to dry for a few hours in the sun before brushing it off. Before eating, make sure to thoroughly wash the carrots.

## Saving of Seeds

This means that parsnips and carrots develop seeds in their second year of life. In the first year of their life, they store energy in the root of the plant. These plants, if left in the ground throughout winter, will come back to life in the spring with gorgeous umbel flowers that look much like Queen Anne's lace. We can trace our domesticated carrots back to Queen Anne's lace because it is a wild variety of the vegetable.

Carrot seed can be saved using isolation techniques, but they aren't necessary for parsnips, which are insect-pollinated and widely dispersed. There is also the possibility of inbreeding depression, thus it is best to save seeds from a population of at least twenty plants to avoid this issue.

When the umbels have not yet blossomed, bag them to keep insects away (using spun polyester material, such as what you can buy as a floating row cover). All the umbels need not be bagged, but only one from each plant that you intend to use as seed. A horsehair or camel hair brush is an effective tool for cross-pollination once the umbels have bloomed. Once the blooms have formed, the procedure is as simple as removing the bags from as many as you can maintain free of insects each day for two to four weeks. Each umbel's blooms should be gently brushed with the brush, travelling back and forth so that all of the umbel's flowers are covered. Continue until all umbels have been processed by removing the bags from each umbel and replacing them with new ones.

Cut the umbels from the plant when they are two weeks old and store them in a cool, dry location. By rubbing the umbels with your hands, you can remove the seeds, which can then be winnowed to remove the chaff.

the procedure for preparing and preserving

In wet sand or peat moss, entire carrots and parsnips can be kept in the pantry for a few months. A half-inch above the root, the tips are trimmed so that they don't draw moisture away from the roots. Alternatively, they can be blanched for four minutes and then either chilled and dried and preserved or dehydrated. A sealed package of dry beans will keep for a few months in the refrigerator.

Pickles of Carrots and Parsnips

Ingredients:

- Carrots weighing one pound

At least one-pound of parsnips

- 312 quarts of distilled white vinegar
- 1 and a half cups of sugar
- 2 tsp ground cinnamon per serving

The following ingredients: • 1 teaspoon of ground allspice

- 1 tsp of sea salt or other non-iodized salt —

Garlic cloves: • 12 teaspoon

Procedure:

Cut the carrots and parsnips into spears of 312 inches long by quartering them lengthwise. Clean pint jars should be used to store the chutney in. In a saucepan, combine the other ingredients and bring to a boil over medium heat for about five minutes. Fill the jars with this mixture, making sure to cover the spears fully and provide a headspace of 12 inch. For 15 minutes, process the two-piece lids in a boiling water canner.

Carrots with a Lemon Dill Dressing

Ingredients:

Carrots, 1 pound

Lemon, a solitary

- 3 tbsp oil of walnuts (butter can be substituted)

Tsp. of dried dill herb (about one-half teaspoon)

Procedure:

The oven should be preheated to 350 degrees Fahrenheit. Cut the carrots into equal-sized pieces, drizzle with walnut oil, and then top with dill weed and a quarter of the lemon zest and juice (remove any pits). Spread out in a single layer in a baking dish that is covered. Allow to bake for 30 minutes, or until easily pierced with a fork.

# Chapter Eight

# CORN

Everything from cornstarch baby powder to ethanol for vehicles is made from maize, one of the largest commercial crops in the country. There are many genetically engineered foods out there. Between 79% and 95% of the maize cultivated in the United States is genetically modified, with the percentage varying by state.

Europe currently prohibits the import or cultivation of genetically modified corn for human consumption because of concerns about its safety. I can't say for sure if they're safe or not, so I won't. A lot of the information about its dangers is overly pessimistic, whereas the information about its safety comes from sources that are more objective. The weirdest development in this discussion has been the approval of federal rules that supersede state laws requiring the labelling of items containing genetically modified crops..

There's no way to tell if the food you're eating contains genetically modified organisms except from rules prohibiting the use of genetically modified seeds in USDA organic products.

As previously said, the facts on the safety or harm of genetically modified corn is quite hazy in my opinion. It is the only way to guarantee that the corn you eat is free of genetically altered traits other than purchasing pricey organic-labeled items.

Varieties

As a result of the widespread usage of maize as a staple food in many regions of the world, a wide variety of corn products have been developed. It is possible to grind flour corn into a fine powder. Coarse cornmeal is made from flint corn. Dent corn is a byproduct of the feed and industrial industries. Popcorn is a common ingredient in the preparation of popcorn. The most popular form of corn cultivated at home is sweet corn.

Floriani Red Flint is one of the most productive open-pollinated kinds of flint corn that is currently available. Per 4′ x 8′ bed, you should expect to get about five pounds of grain. Heritable Blue Hopi has an eye-catching hue and a mouthwatering flavour, but it's less productive, yielding only four pounds per 4-foot-by-8-foot bed.

Genetics classify sweet corn as either "normally sugary," "sugary enhanced," or "super-sweet" (Sh2). For example, these genes control the kernel's sugar content and how long the sugar will remain in the kernel before converting into starch. Sweet corn is a recessive feature that evolved from flint or dent corn via natural selection. Sweet corn should be kept at least 400 yards apart from field corns that may be pollinating at the same time because of the recessive nature of these features. Sweet corn kernels won't be sweet if they don't have the right amount of sugar in them.

The oldest sweet corns are Su sweet corns. This genetic profile can be found in nearly all commercially marketed open-pollinated cultivars of sweet corn. Golden Bantam (yellow), Country Gentleman (white), Stowell's Evergreen (white), and Double Standard are popular open-pollinated examples (bicolor). Early Sunglow (yellow), Silver Queen (white), and Butter and Sugar are just a few examples of hybrids featuring Su genes (bicolor).

As long as you don't get too close to each other in terms of distance, you're good to go. Once the ear is plucked from the stalk, sugar begins to convert to starch, so it is imperative that it be processed within thirty minutes of harvest. Su varieties, on the other hand, have a typical corn flavour and can withstand blanching and freezing on the cob.

As a result, Se sweet corn can be kept fresh for up to four days in the refrigerator if properly refrigerated. All commercially marketed Se types are hybrids, despite some attempts underway to produce open-pollinated Se varieties3. Se corn has a great flavour, but because it is so fragile, it doesn't process well. Fresh food is preferable. Kandy Korn (yellow), Argent (white), and Precious Gem are among of the most popular Se types (bicolor).

Sh2 sweet corn may keep its sugar content for up to ten days following harvest, making it an excellent choice for transport by truck and retail display. In addition, the stronger kernels are better able to withstand severe handling, even though they are more suited for transportation than eating. In order to avoid starchy kernels, commercially available Sh2 varieties must be kept apart from Se and Su varieties. Yellow Challenger, white Aspen, and red Dazzle are all popular Sh2 cultivars (bicolor).

Since planting depth and soil temperature fluctuation are more of a factor in small farming than most other options, I suggest sticking with Su and Se cultivars. Open-pollinated types, all of which are Su strains, are the only ones that may be saved for seed. Floriani Red Flint or Blue Hopi for cornmeal, and Golden Bantam or Stowell's Evergreen for sweet corn are good starter selections; you'll likely find other types that you enjoy via experimenting.

## Preparing the Soil

A lot of food, light, and water are required for corn to produce to its full potential. In addition, because of its thin root system, it necessitates meticulous soil care. Ideally, organic matter should be tilled into the soil's top six to eight inches, with a pH range of 6.0 to 6.5. Heavy feeder, it is treated with high-nitrogen fertilisers three times during the season in agribusiness production. " They employ highly soluble synthetic fertilisers and neglect to keep soil organic matter levels high enough to hang on to those nutrients, which explains why this is the case. There is no need to apply fertiliser to a well-prepared bed in order to yield excellent maize.

Mix in at least six cubic feet of mature compost for every forty-eight square feet of bed, then rake it into the soil. Lime can be used to raise the pH to between 6.0 and 6.5. Using sea mineral solids, add micronutrients at the manufacturer's suggested rate. Based on the results of a home soil test for nitrogen, phosphorous, and potassium, add organic fertiliser to the soil. Finally, add ten pounds of alfalfa meal and two pounds of blood meal every forty-eight-square-foot bed in addition to the nitrogen you've previously added depending on a soil test to offer additional slow and fast release nitrogen. In order to keep the nutrients in the soil, the compost will work with them to keep the rain from washing them away and making them available to the corn. Since I started using this technique, I've never had to worry about fertiliser again.

## Preparation and Seeding

Hybrid Sh2 types of corn, in particular, can be fickle when it comes to planting depth, temperature, water level, and other factors. Staggered germination, seeds that perish in the ground before sprouting, and other problems can affect even Su varieties.

Unlike the agri-giant Monsanto, a small farm can benefit greatly from this solution: start your seeds indoors one week before the last frost instead of putting them directly in the ground. Then, one week after the last frost, plant out your corn seedlings at one-foot spacing in all directions. You can avoid all of these issues if you regularly engage in this technique, resulting in a neat, uniform stand of corn.

Plant your seeds one inch deep, twelve inches apart, one week after the last frost and water them every day until they sprout.

Wait a week after the corn seedlings have sprouted before planting the beans if you follow my method of planting them together (see Mini Farming). Otherwise, your corn will be overshadowed by the beans as they begin to grow.

Corn is pollinated by the wind and has a significant tendency to crossbreed. When the ears are pollinated, the kernels will form. When the pollen-bearing tops have grown, I reach in and gently shake a few corn plants every now and then to disseminate the pollen. Planting the corn tightly spaced usually suffices.

## diseases, weeds, and other pests

Weeds are a major issue for corn production on large farms with robotic harvesting, which can cover hundreds of acres. The herbicides are sprayed in large quantities, and genetically modified corn that is resistant to the herbicides is sown. Weeds are easy to manage on a small farm because of the scale. It's enough to just hand-weed or use a stirrup hoe between plants if you remove all the weeds before planting.

While insect issues abound in commercial monoculture, a professionally operated tiny farm that practises crop sanitation and rotation has only a few noticeable pests that can be easily controlled. The defoliation of corn by Japanese beetles can have a negative impact on yield. Lawn grubs like Japanese beetles are all over the place. Treating your entire lawn and beds with milky spore disease once the disease has been entrenched in a year or two can be a useful preventative if you have a lot of land so that there is a good buffer with your neighbours. Traps for Japanese beetles, which may be purchased at hardware stores, can be effective, but they must be set at least 100 feet away from a garden.

Beetles from Japan are attracted to one another. In order to keep them under control, one option is to pick them up one at a time and place them in a soapy bucket. You can probably avoid the problem altogether if you pick them off regularly as soon as you detect them. Sprays like pyrethrin and rotenone, when used as directed, can help control them, although this is a last choice due to the high cost of these products.

Corn earworm is another common pest. An unremarkable moth's larva can be seen here. Aphids can inflict damage on just about any edible plant in the garden except for corn, which will not show any signs of attack until after harvest. Even though winds can carry the moth up to Canada and do significant damage in the South, the moth can't overwinter north of Maryland.

The speck-sized eggs of this moth are laid on maize silk by the moth itself. A little worm emerges from the hatching eggs and digs its way into the ear canal. By the time you're done eating, it will have grown to a solid three inches in length. Because it looks like a kernel of corn with its head, it may go undetected for a while because it has bored through the cob and replaced its head there. Having a worm hanging out of your mouth after chomping down on corn might be unnerving! The worm can also simply chew along the ear's outer edge. It usually consumes portion of the silk, preventing the pollination and growth of the kernels.

Bt (Bacillus thuringiensis) mixed with supermarket corn oil and liquid lecithin (available at health food stores) as an emulsifier can significantly reduce maize earworm damage. Lecithin and Bt (in this case, DiPel DF) should be mixed with one quart of maize oil and one heaping spoonful of liquid lecithin. The mixture should be well incorporated. Apply 0.5 cc of the liquid to each of the corn tassels, then shake well. To get a precise reading, I use a little syringe (without the needle) that I purchased from a veterinary supply store. Hand-distribute it on the corn tassel to provide a uniform coating.

Pollination may be harmed by the oil, but it is particularly efficient in preventing earworm damage while it is still in the critical stage of development. Within a 5- to 8-day window, pollination will not be affected and the product will still be effective. This stage begins fifty-seven days from the start of silk growth, or thirty-four days after the silk is fully grown, whichever comes first.

It's possible that such an observation isn't possible. However, hope does not yet fade away! When the silk's tips are just beginning to brown and wilt, that's a good time to apply the oil. Corn kernels are only covered with silk for about an inch or so of their length when you remove their husk.

This is the best way to get the most control while using the least amount of materials. That said, it's possible it won't work. Raising a lot of maize can soon become a laborious task. Use a Bt- or spinosad-based product according to the label guidelines and spray the corn well once a week with an ordinary garden sprayer starting when the silk has formed. As long as you don't skip, the water-based spray will keep appropriate control with no negative effects on pollination.

There are a dozen diseases of commercial consequence in large-scale corn growing, but at a tiny farm where soil fertility is maintained, crops are cycled among beds and crop debris is properly composted none of them are likely to be a problem. In the same way, machinery damage to the cornstalks or ears is a major cause of many of the diseases that plague the agricultural industry. This won't be an issue with small farming approaches because they don't make use of machineries. Changing to hybrid Su corn for future plants may solve disease problems even if effective cultural practises haven't.

Even while lodging of corn isn't a pest or disease problem in and of itself, it can have a negative impact on large-scale production and even on a tiny farm. When a stalk breaks below the ear, it is called lodging, and it is frequently caused by strong winds. Because mini-farm corn is grown in beds, lodging can be completely prevented by screwing some four-foot uprights to the corners of the bed using deck screws and running some strong string resistant to UV degradation around the bed and through holes drilled near the top of the uprights' uprights'

## Harvest

At the end of the growing season, field corns such as dent and flint corn are gathered and sold. Gather as soon as the green husk turns tan, and then twist the ear slightly while holding the cornstalk in one hand and tugging it down with the other. The husks and as much silk as possible should be removed as soon as possible from the ears. Finally, the ears should be kept out of the rain and wind for as long as possible in a place with sufficient air circulation. The kernels can be removed from the cobs by shelling once the kernels have dried. Even on a small scale, you can use gloves to avoid blisters and rub two ears together to twist the cob in your hands to remove dry kernels from ears. To dry even more, gather the kernels and place them in a container out of direct sunlight. If you're looking for something more substantial, you can use a mechanical sheller or a hand sheller. These mechanical shellers are a lot of fun to use because they are powered by hand cranks. A mechanical sheller was a lot of fun for my cousins and I to use to shell corn for my grandfather. The fact that he had never instructed us to do it meant we had no idea it was work.

Harvesting sweet corn at the right time of year is more difficult. The kernels are improperly developed and the sugar content is inadequate if you harvest them too early. Corn that is harvested too late gets hard and starchy. When it comes to open-pollinated kinds, the ears don't all mature at the same time. As a result, large-scale farmers increasingly turn to hybrids, which make it possible to harvest an entire crop of corn in a single go. However, open-pollinated sweet corn ears can all be harvested within a week of each other.

There is a wide variation in the “days to harvest” reported in seed catalogues based on factors such as temperature, sunlight, and water availability. At twenty-one days after the silk appears, begin inspecting the ears. Feel the ears to determine if they are solid when the silk has turned brown and is beginning to dry. Assuming this is the case, gently detach a small section of the husk from the ear about halfway down and puncture a kernel with your thumb. The corn isn’t ready yet if the juice is clear. To harvest, the juice must be milky. The corn is overripe if it is creamy. As long as the sweet corn is a little overripe, it’s perfectly suited for canning.

Harvest the ears as you would for field corn, but keep the husks on for decoration. The best way to keep sugar from turning into starch is to keep the product in a refrigerator until it’s time to utilise it. Use or store Su variety within a few hours of harvesting. You have two to three days with Se variations. You get a full week with Sh2 variety.

## Saving of Seeds

To avoid inbreeding depression, a large number of plants must be used as the breeding pool for corn, which is an outbreeding plant. In the case of corn, it may not even be possible to save seed on a small scale because so many plants are required. Plants that are visibly inferior or off-type should be culled from at least 200. Keeping pure seed corn from cross-pollination with other corn varieties is best done by keeping it at least a mile apart from other corn kinds, if not more.

There are two ways to harvest field corn seeds: one is by hand, and the other is by machine. In order to save seed from sweet corn, treat it like field corn and allow the ear to reach maturity rather than picking at its milk stage. Corn should be shelled into a large container, mixed thoroughly, and a random sample of at least a quart taken from the container should be used as seed, according to my recommendation. Cornmeal can be made from the dried sweet corn left over after seed has been harvested.

the procedure for preparing and preserving

A cold, dry environment with an airtight container is the best location to keep dried corn. In order to keep pests at bay, that container should be completely oxygen-free. This can be done in a variety of ways. It's possible, but it's time-consuming, to place a metal plate over the corn and then add dry ice (solidified carbon dioxide). All of the oxygen will be displaced by carbon dioxide as the gas vaporises due to its weight. Put the cover on the container when the dry ice is nearly gone.

You can also use an airtight metal container, a heatproof plate on top of the corn, an unscented candle on top of it, and a cover. The ratio of oxygen to carbon dioxide will be altered in such a way that it is harmful to animal existence even if all of the oxygen is not removed. Each time the lid is opened, you'll need to relight the candle. Using a hand grinder with proper burrs, such as the Corona grain mill, flint and dent corn can be ground into truly exceptional cornmeal.

To prevent sugars from being converted to starches, sweet corn should be cooked as soon as possible after harvest. Sweet corn on the cob is the most common method of consumption. The ears of corn are boiled for twenty minutes or so after they've been shushed. For me, it's all about the butter and salt. But there are plenty of other options available. Grilled corn on the cob is another option. The husk should be peeled back but left connected. The silk should be removed. The kernels should be generously oiled before the husk is returned and tied shut with cotton string. Then cook for 15 to 20 minutes, turning frequently, over a medium-hot grill. Wrap the ears in aluminium foil and use butter instead of oil if you don't want to deal with the husk.

On or off the cob, sweet corn can be frozen. Four minutes of blanching, four minutes of cooling, four minutes of drying, and four minutes of putting in freezer bags that have been vacuumed. In addition to blanching, blanched corn can also be dehydrated off of the cob. When harvested a few days late, sweet corn holds up well to pressure canning.

Corn in Cans

Ingredients:

Each pint contains 2 pounds of husked corn on the cob

- Salt
- Water

Procedure:

Remove the silk from the corn by husking it. Cut the kernels from the cob with a sharp knife. Pour boiling water over the corn in the jars leaving an inch of headspace, and process in a pressure canner at 10 pounds of pressure for 55 minutes for pints or 1 hour and 20 minutes for quarts. Optionally add 12 teaspoon salt per pint or 1 teaspoon salt per quart.

a delicious salsa made with fresh corn

Ingredients:

fresh sweet corn, 5 ounces

A jalapeo pepper is required.

- 12 pound of tomatillos or tomatoes (recommended)

1 red pepper, cut into small pieces and the membranes removed

The onion should be thinly cut.

Lemon, a solitary

Ground coriander: • 12 tsp

Chopped fresh cilantro: • 1 tbsp

• Water

Procedure:

Cut the corn kernels from the cobs after they have been husked. Remove the jalapeo pepper's membranes and slice it into small pieces. Remove the husks from the tomatillos before chopping them. Cook over medium heat, adding just enough water to prevent burning but not enough to overcook the ingredients in a frying pan with the lemon juice squeezed into it. Remove from heat after 5 minutes of constant stirring. Before serving, add the cilantro and chill in the refrigerator. This is a fresh salsa and should not be canned because it lacks the necessary acidity.

CPSIA information can be obtained
at www.ICGtesting.com
Printed in the USA
LVHW061836130722
723448LV00014B/180

9 781804 768358